CW00819674

THE LITTLE BOOK OF
OASIS
INSULTS

The hilarious and unofficial book of Gallagher brothers' quotes

Jake James

spruce

Stay young and invincible Branski,
for you are the ultimate madhead.

First published in Great Britain in 2025 by Spruce, an imprint of
Octopus Publishing Group Ltd
Carmelite House, 50 Victoria Embankment,
London EC4Y 0DZ
www.octopusbooks.co.uk

An Hachette UK Company
www.hachette.co.uk

The authorized representative in the EEA is Hachette Ireland,
8 Castlecourt Centre, Dublin 15, D15 XTP3, Ireland (email: info@hbgi.ie)

Text copyright © Jake James 2025
Illustrations copyright © Simon Spilsbury 2025

Distributed in the US by Hachette Book Group,
1290 Avenue of the Americas, 4th and 5th Floors
New York, NY 10104

Distributed in Canada by Canadian Manda Group,
664 Annette St., Toronto, Ontario, Canada M6S 2C8

ISBN 978 1 84601 596 0

A CIP catalogue record for this book is available from the British Library.

Typeset in 10/16pt Heldane Text by Jouve (UK), Milton Keynes

Printed and bound in Great Britain.
13 5 7 9 10 8 6 4 2

MIX
Paper | Supporting
responsible forestry
FSC
www.fsc.org
FSC® C104740

CONTENTS

INTRODUCTION

Hello and welcome to *The Little Book of Oasis Insults*, now do f*ck off. Or keep reading if you want to experience some of the funniest invective ever aimed in the direction of Adele, Prince Harry, Gary Neville and aliens. In compiling the best insults from Liam and Noel Gallagher there is almost too much material to choose from because they have been slagging off each other and everyone else for 30 years. In fact, this compendium could have been *the* Giant *Book of Oasis Insults* but the cost of paper skyrocketed this year.

It's hard to think of anyone else who's come up with enough funny insults to fill a book. Maybe Donald Trump? Although just putting a snide word in front an enemy's first name isn't the summit of high wit. Groucho Marx? Except that some of his jibes might come over as a little on the creaky side these days. Shakespeare? OK, maybe you'll understand some of them if you're doing A' Level English. But just imagine trying to fill a book with insults from one of Oasis's rock rivals. If this was a collection of Chris Martin's *Best Barbs and Comebacks*, the cost of paper wouldn't be an issue.

So, let's get into why Liam and Noel are the masters of the insult. It's down to three simple facts:

1) They are honest

2) They enjoy it

3) They are funny

They are honest

I need to be myself, I can't be no one else . . . is the first line of Oasis's debut single 'Supersonic'. Noel wrote it, Liam sang it and it's fair to say they've both stuck to that philosophy in all their interviews since.

And there have been a lot of interviews. No one gives such great copy as the Gallaghers. Noel and Liam are dream interviewees because, when they are asked a question, they answer it. Plus they answer in a way that celebs are told they can't answer a question anymore – in an unguarded and candid way. As Liam said on Radio X in 2024, 'I don't VAR what comes out of my mouth, man. Whatever comes out comes out and I live and die by it.'

If we're lucky their answers can tip over into the outrageous and inflammatory. In fact, the brothers have no problem rocking the boat, upsetting the apple cart and frightening the horses all in one sarcastic put-down. No one is going to describe the Gallaghers as mealy-mouthed.

Here's how Liam sees it (as told to *The Times* in June 2017):

> *We've had enough of politician rock'n'rollers who*
> *say all the right things before going back to their nice*
> *houses. I'm the truth juice, man. I'm a little aggy*
> *bastard and that's what it's all about.*

The brothers pride themselves on never dodging a question, however personal, contentious or idiotic; if you're a fan of hearing 'no comment', try Channel 4's *24 Hours in Police Custody*. If anyone at a record company has ever attempted to give Liam media training, well, let's hope they recorded it and one day the footage is leaked.

Noel, similarly, sees it as his duty to give a full and frank response to any enquiry. 'If someone wants to know what I think of Adele, I'll f*cking tell them,' he once said, and then proceeded to slag Adele off, despite not having been invited to. And here he is making the point again in *The Guardian* in 2008, regarding one of his favourite targets, Keane:

> *. . . well, if somebody asks me what I think of Keane,*
> *I'll tell 'em. I don't like 'em. I'll obviously take it a*
> *step too far and grossly insult the keyboard player's*
> *mam or summat, but I'm afraid that's just me.*

Liam and Noel would baulk at using such therapy-speak buzzwords as 'present' and 'authentic', but both terms describe them well. Yes, they can be blunt, even brutal . . . but audiences respond to the their honesty, which they don't get from many others in the public eye. Maybe Miriam Margolyes and Danny Dyer are in the same mould, but they can't get a stadium full of Brazilians to belt out 'Wonderwall'.

They enjoy it

When the Beatles hit the US in 1964, America fell in love with their vibrancy and wit. However, as they publicized their final US tour, in 1966, the Fab Four were sullen and defensive, worn down by the repetitive, moronic and loaded questions that were being put to them.

Rather than two years, Liam and Noel have been at it for three decades. Yet the sheer pleasure they still take in answering daft questions comes through on the screen, over the radio or off the page. As Noel told the *Grantland* blog in 2011:

> *I've never understood musicians who don't enjoy doing promotional interviews. I just can't believe it. I always think, 'Your life must have been so brilliant before you were in a band.'*

The Gallaghers can face repetitive, moronic and loaded questions all day long without breaking a sweat. Which is incredible when one considers that they have been mocked, misquoted and taken out of context for over 30 years. In fact, they are that rare breed of celebrity who appears delighted to be doing any publicity, relishing the opportunity to turn the same-old-shit questions into gleaming Gallagher-ized comedy gold. Most stars moan about the slog of promotion and answering questions all day, but Noel loves it. In fact, when asked by *Esquire* in 2015 what his hobby was, he replied,

> *Doing interviews. I f*cking love it. I could do this all day long. It's sick . . . Because I get to be a gobshite.*

Now some might argue that the Gallaghers are just putting on a show, tossing out insults at all and sundry in order to get headlines. There is, of course, an element of truth to this. It's said that, at the beginning of their career, when Oasis began to do press, Noel would ask journalists pre-interview, 'Right, who do you want me to slag off?' If he did, and it certainly sounds like Noel, was he being a shrewd operator who was hungry for headlines or was he enjoying the sport of it all and his ability to deliver zingers to order?

Also we should bear in mind Noel's very fair point, made in *Shortlist* magazine in 2011:

> *You can say that you respect someone as an artist a thousand times and it will never get reported. But you call someone a c*nt once . . .*

I suppose a good test of how much Liam and Noel enjoy bandying around insults is whether they do it off the clock. Do they take the piss out of other bands when no one is actually inviting them to? Well, if there's any truth to the following story that's all over the internet, Jon Bon Jovi, whose band Oasis fell out with many years ago, has something he'd like to share:

> *Liam Gallagher was giving me nuisance phone calls for over a decade. God knows how he got my number. He would ring at three or four in the morning just to tell me my music was shit . . . Sometimes he would call me the bastard son of Richard Branson, and other times he would shout 'Lionhead' down the phone until I hung up. In the end, I offered to pay him $500,000, and begged him to stop. He told me to 'Eat shit' . . .*

Whether this happened or not is impossible to say.

Although I hope it's legit, as it shows that even in their downtime the Gallaghers are well up for high-end inter-rockstar trolling, which is incredibly heartening to hear.

Finally let's talk about their humour

There are over a hundred funny insults in this book, but there could have easily been two hundred more . . . In an interview situation Liam and Noel are head and shoulders above most comedians. If you think that's overstating the case, here's one of the greatest comedians in the world, Bill Burr, musing about Oasis on his *Monday Morning* podcast in July 2023:

> *Not only were they one of the great bands of all time, those two f*cking guys are arguably two of the best comedians that Britain ever produced. As a stand-up comic to listen to their interviews, read them and watch them, it is annoying how f*cking funny they are.*

Let's investigate their styles. Similar to his belief in his own musical talents, Noel seems to have complete faith in his comic powers. Put him in front of a mic and he's relaxed, confident and effortlessly funny, tossing out droll rambling anecdotes and hilarious turns of phrase like he's the Peter Ustinov of Burnage.

Liam, as we all know, has a different edge – less smooth and more fragmented. If we were going to compare him to another regular Michael Parkinson guest, he'd be closer to Spike Milligan . . . in a parka. Liam's more crazy, more volatile and with a genuine gift for the dark and surreal. When Liam gets on a good rant . . . it's like he's improvising a new verse for *I Am the Walrus*.

Here he is talking to *GQ* in 1998, after George Harrison had slagged him off:

Isn't It a Pity? It will be when I meet George Harrison. I'm gonna stand on his head and play golf. I'm gonna do me Roy Castle impersonation on his head . . . I had a dream where I drop-kicked him in the throat, George, and smashed McCartney from here to Jupiter and back. He didn't have his seatbelt on. My name is disturbance . . . And there'll be no big chaps around, man. Just me and me dick, man. And I'll hit him with me knob.

One of the extraordinary things about that little speech (apart from the fact he's talking about one of his heroes) is that Liam didn't swear. However, in that respect, it's a bit of an outlier. In this book you'll be lucky to find a Liam or Noel quote that isn't laced with profanity, which Noel puts down to their mother Peggy; as he told *Esquire* in 2015;

Hard work and a f*cking filthy tongue, that's what I inherited from my mum. She taught the Nineties how to swear.

Well, we thank Peggy Gallagher for that, as well as for grounding Noel so often that he decided to pick up a guitar.

Before reading this book, you may be of the mind that Oasis are the greatest rock band in the world. Or you may not. However, after reading this book, you will agree that they are the greatest rock band in the world . . . at being funny. And if you don't, as Noel observed, 'You gotta roll with it, as some idiot once said.' ('Oasis special', *The O-Zone*, BBC, 1995)

Chapter 1

NOEL ON LIAM –
MY BIG MOUTH

There's a great tradition of fraternal rivalry in rock, from the Kinks' Ray and Dave Davies trading punches just before taking the stage to the Everly Brothers refusing to talk to each other after their shows. But there's never been a pair like Liam and Noel. They've been scrapping since day dot and they'll happily take chunks out of each other whether they are in a band together or not.

Noel's always had a problem with Liam. Noel has admitted that he thinks Liam is cooler, funnier and better looking than him, so it might be down to that. On the other hand, Liam's admitted that as a teenager he once got home drunk and pissed all over Noel's new stereo, so that's also a possibility.

'Liam got a Rolex. I got a Rolls Royce.
Which is brilliant, cos I can't drive
and Liam can't tell the time.'

(*The Jonathan Ross Show*,
BBC1, September 2004)

'I can read him and I can f*cking play him like a slightly disused arcade game. I can make him make decisions that he thinks are his, but really they're mine.'

(*SPIN*, October 2005)

'I don't think I've ever been so embarrassed for a man in my entire life . . . walking around in what looks like a pair of my son's pyjamas, shouting into a mic about some perceived injustice . . . If you can't sing 'em, don't play 'em!'

(*Guardian*, August 2019)

Asked about Liam's new solo career:

'I've heard . . . the one that sounds like Adele shouting into a bucket.'

(*i-D*, November 2017)

'He's the angriest man you'll
ever meet. He's like a man with
a fork in a world of soup.'

(Q, April 2009)

'I read these interviews with him and I don't know who the guy is who's in these interviews, he seems really cool, because the guy I've been in a band with for the last 18 years is a f*cking knobhead.'

(*Herald Sun*, October 2008)

'He says, "Why have you got a
fork in that bottle of champagne?"
I replied, "Cos it keeps the bubbles,
keeps it fresh . . ." A few weeks
later we were round his house and
opened the fridge door and there
was a spoon in a bottle of milk.'

(BBC Radio 6 Music, November 2012)

'I'm trying to soar like an eagle,
an eagle, and I'm being asked
to comment on the ramblings
of a common pigeon.'

(Q, December 2017)

'Liam believes in the Tooth Fairy
and the Loch Ness Monster,
so I'm afraid he's not a
very reliable witness.'

(interview with Dave Fanning for
RTÉ 2FM, June 2023)

On Liam's solo work:

'I think it's unsophisticated music. For unsophisticated people. Made by an unsophisticated man.'

(*Guardian*, August 2019)

'He's the man who puts the "tit" in attitude.'

(Studio 68 on XFM, July 2000)

Chapter 2

LIAM ON NOEL – HEADSHRINKER

Fans of the Gallaghers' back-and-forth barbs should give thanks to their mum, who made Liam and Noel share a bedroom, while their older brother Paul got his own. That domestic decision fostered an intense mutual antagonism that has played out in public to this day, in the form of hilariously blunt disses and surreal put-downs.

Yet even when the Gallaghers are slinging around the most vicious slights and slurs and the world is getting concerned, you sense that they are doing it foremost not to hurt but to amuse each other. OK, maybe that's overstating it. Hurt *and* amuse.

Anyway, let's hear what Liam has to say about Noel. As a member of the Oasis management team once beautifully put it, 'Noel has a lot of buttons and Liam has a lot of fingers.'

'That's why we'll be the best band in the world, because I f*ckin' hate that twat there . . . I f*ckin' hate him. And I hope one day there's a release where I can smash the f*ck out of him, with a f*ckin' Rickenbacker, right on his nose.'

(*Wibbling Rivalry* interview
with John Harris, April 1994)

'He couldn't handle the rock 'n' roll. He was too scared of it. So now he's gone all cosmic pop and Leo Sayer.'

(Radio X, 2019)

'I like Noel outside the band . . .
I f*cking adore him and
I'd do anything for him.
But the geezer that's in this
f*cking business, he's one of the
biggest cocks in the universe.'

(*NME*, June 2013)

'He said we had a year to come up
with a band name and came up with
Beady Eye. He had three and came
up with the High Flying Turds.
I don't know who dressed him but he
looks like something out of Westlife.'

(Q, 2011)

'Every time I see pictures of him,
I just see a potato . . . a stalker potato
when he has his arm around Bono.'

(*The Howard Stern Show*, July 2017)

'Every f*cking soundcheck
he'd stand in the middle
and sing. The geezer's got
small-man syndrome.'

(Q, August 2016)

'That c*nt can't even f*cking
sell out Apollo in Manchester –
3,000 capacity in his own
f*cking town, the f*cking
embarrassing f*cking donut.'

(NME, February 2020)

'I'd rather eat my own shit
than be in a band with him again.
He's a miserable little f*ck,
if you know what I mean.'

(*LA Weekly*, December 2011)

'He's in one of his really, really, really, big houses, probably eating tofu, while having a f*cking face peel. Ain't that right, man of the people?'

(*Sky News*, October 2016)

'Stick your thousand pounds right up your f*ckin' arse 'til it comes out your f*ckin' big toe.'

(*Wibbling Rivalry* interview with John Harris, April 1994)

Chapter 3

OASIS ON THE HEROES FROM THE PAST – DON'T LOOK BACK IN ANGER

The Gallagher brothers have always paid tribute to their musical heroes of the Sixties and Seventies. Noel declared on *Desert Island Discs* that if he ever met Pink Floyd's Roger Waters, he would lick his face in honour of what a fan he is. Meanwhile Liam is so obsessed with John Lennon that for a while he believed he was the iconic Beatle reincarnated. The only problem being Liam was born eight years before Lennon died. However, as we have already seen Liam taking a few shots at George Harrison, we know that when the Gallaghers are in battle mode, they have no problem turning their guns on the old guard.

**Liam on Mick Jagger and
Keith Richards:**

'Dirty old nipple. Sweaty old
mushroom.'

(*GQ*, February 1998)

Liam on Keith Richard and George Harrison:

'They're jealous and senile and not getting enough f*cking meat pies.'

(*Sun*, October 1997)

Noel:

'You don't have to be great to be successful. Look at Phil Collins.'

(quoted in *Observer*, April 2013)

Noel:

'Look. I was a superhero in the '90s.
I said so at the time. McCartney,
Weller, Townshend, Richards,
my first album's better than
all their first albums.
Even they'd admit that.'

(*Guardian*, November 2006)

Noel on Brian Wilson of the Beach Boys:

'Who would want to be Brian Wilson,
sitting in a studio in a nappy,
eating a f*cking carrot with
your little fat feet in a sandpit,
not going on tour? F*ck that.'

(*Rolling Stone*, February 2015)

Noel on solo artists:

'Solo artists are generally totally insane. Elton John? Slightly eccentric. George Michael? He's mad as custard.'

(*New York Times*, November 2011)

Liam:

'I have never seen a U2 fan.
I have never seen anyone with a
U2 shirt or been around
someone's house that has a f*cking
U2 record. Where do their fans
f*cking come from?'

(Interview with Chris Sullivan, March 2010)

Noel on U2:

'Play 'One', shut the
f*ck up about Africa.'

(*Daily Telegraph*, February 2007)

Liam:

You see pictures of Bono
running around LA with his
little white legs and a bottle of
Volvic and he looks like a fanny.
I mean, maybe if it was a
bottle of vodka.'

(*Observer*, June 2002)

Noel on Paul Weller:

'People think he's some deep god,
but he's a moany old bastard. He's
like Victor Meldrew with a suntan.'

(*NME*, June 1995)

Chapter 4

OASIS ON THEIR ROCK GROUP RIVALS – ROLL WITH IT

US comedy legend Carl Reiner once noted it was sad that the public didn't really get to see how hilarious Mel Brooks could be, as Mel was at his funniest when he was slagging off other comedians privately. Fortunately, Liam and Noel have no problem eviscerating their rock group rivals, *publicly*. While modern groups seem loath to criticize their rivals and are all the more boring for it, we sense that the Gallaghers are still itching to slag off Scouting for Girls and will do so even if the interviewer asks them, 'How do you take your tea?'

Noel on Blur:

'The thing that gets me is, people will say that [Blur's] the Beatles and we're the Stones. The fact of the matter is, we're the Beatles and the Stones, and they're the f*cking Monkees.'

(*CMJ*, April 1996)

Liam:

'Chris Martin looks like a geography teacher. What's all that with writing messages about Free Trade? If he wants to write things down I'll give him a pen and a pad of paper. Bunch of students.'

(*Sun*, 2003)

Noel:

'I feel sorry for Keane.
No matter how hard they try
they'll always be squares. Even
if one of them started injecting
heroin into his cock people
would go, "Yeah, but your dad
was a vicar, good night".'

(*Herald Sun*, October 2008)

Liam:

'I mean, the devil's got all the good gear. What's God got? The Inspiral Carpets and nuns. F*ck that.'

(quoted in Paul Lester, *Oasis: The Illustrated Story*, Hamlyn, 1997)

Liam on Mumford & Sons:

'Everyone looks like they've got f*cking nits and eat lentil soup with their sleeves rolled up!'

(*Q* magazine, 2012)

Noel on Keane:

'Traditionally speaking, the three biggest twats in any band are the singer, the keyboardist and the drummer. I don't need to say anything else.'

(NME.com, 2005)

Noel:

'I did drugs for 18 years and
I never got that bad as to say,
"You know what? I think the
Kaiser Chiefs are brilliant." '

(*The Chris Moyles Show*,
BBC Radio 1, August 2008)

Liam on Radiohead's *The King of Limbs*:

'I like to think that what we do, we do f*cking well. Them writing a song about a f*cking tree? Give me a f*cking break! A thousand year old tree? Go f*ck yourself!'

(*Quietus*, February 2011)

Liam:

'The White Stripes? Fooking rubbish. School ties? At the age of 24? Fooking hell.'

(*NME*, July 2002)

Noel:

'Jack White has just written a song for Coca-Cola. End of. He ceases to be in the club. And he looks like Zorro on doughnuts.'

(*NME*, December 2005)

Chapter 5

OASIS ON POP
STARS – STOP CRYING
YOUR HEART OUT

Liam and Noel don't always go in hard on pop stars. Noel used to be sympathetic to *X Factor* wannabes looking to better their life, although he hated the mawkish sob stories they'd use to curry favour with the public. Meanwhile Liam once outed himself mid-interview as an unlikely fan of S Club Juniors, much to Noel's amusement. Having said that, on a good or a bad day, they are both more than happy to have a pop at pop. Otherwise, how could they take the piss out of a certain 'fat dancer from Take That'?

Noel:

'Adele? I'm not a fan.
She always comes on the radio
when I'm having my cornflakes:
"Hello?" No, f*ck off!'

(*GQ*, March 2016)

Liam on Florence Welch:

'I'm sure she's a nice girl,
but she sounds like someone's
stood on her f*cking foot.'

(*XFM*, February 2010)

Noel:

'Take That's Howard Donald said that he hears voices at night willing him to fail. To fail at what? You don't do anything, Howard.'

(*Irish Examiner*, January 2006)

Noel:

'Why is Posh Beckham writing a f*cking book of her memoirs? She can't even chew chewing gum and walk in a f*cking straight line at the same time, let alone write a book.'

(*NME*, September 2001)

Noel on Madonna:

'Six hours! In a gym! You sleep for eight, right – so that's 14 gone already. What do you do with your one hour off? Do you want to get so supple that you can eventually stick your own head up your arse?'

(*Evening Standard*, 2008)

Noel on Robbie Williams:

'I'd probably kick him down the stairs a couple of times, not that I'm a violent person. I think he needs to be held down by people in white coats and slapped around the face for half an hour. Robbie's the biggest fake ever and yet he thinks he's Elvis.'

(*Now*, May 2002)

Noel:

'Sam Smith just stands there
like Boy George in a coma.'

(*NME*, March 2015)

Noel on Adele:

'Music for f*cking grannies.
Music has nosedived into f*cking
blandness. A sea of cheese.'

(*Music Feeds*, December 2015)

**Noel upon being given a gift-wrapped
40th birthday present on *Soccer AM*:**

'It's not the head of James Blunt,
is it? Is it? I do hope it is.'

(Sky Sports, May 2007)

Noel:

'Kylie Minogue is just a demonic
little idiot as far as I'm concerned.'

(*OK!*, June 2002)

Chapter 6

OASIS ON FOOTBALL – WHERE DID IT ALL GO WRONG?

Liam claimed his only interest up to the age of 18 was football, whereupon someone hit him over the head with a hammer and he got into music. Noel thinks the Premier League is the best thing about Britain, but thankfully it doesn't stop him sticking the boot into specific teams and players. Though they argue about everything else, one thing we do know about Liam and Noel is that they are both lifelong Manchester City fans and will happily take down Man United at any and every opportunity.

Liam, when asked to name
ten things he hates:

'Man United . . . I hate
Man United ten times.'

(source unknown)

**Noel appearing beside Graeme Souness
and Gary Neville on Sky Sports:**

'It's great to be sat beside a legend of
the game . . . and Gary Neville.'

(*Super Sunday*, Sky Sports, December 2017)

Liam on the English football team:

'A bag of shite. My grandmother would do better, on acid with a Toblerone stuck up her arse.'

(interview with Tea Khalifa at Ruisrock festival, Finland, *Jyrki*, MTV3, July 2000)

Noel to Liam:

'Alright. Well if you're proud about getting thrown off ferries, why don't you go and support West Ham and get the f*ck out of my band and go and be a football hooligan.'

(*Wibbling Rivalry* interview with John Harris, April 1994)

Liam on Alex Ferguson:

'Taggart from across the road – he's a top manager and all that but he looks like a dustbin man.'

(*Football365*, January 2010)

Noel on Man United:

'They've had their time.
As an expert of watching a club
with false dawns, I recognize it.'

(*Match of the Day 2*, BBC1, February 2015)

Liam:

'I don't really like the Etihad.
I don't dig it, man, it's like going
and watching the f*cking opera . . .
The last time I seen City I got told to
be quiet by some f*cking donut.'

(*NME*, February 2020)

Noel being interviewed by Ant and Dec:

'If Man City win the league I'd donate
all the proceeds of my next number
one album to charity . . . Can you
make sure they cut that?'

(*CD:UK*, ITV, November 2000)

Noel to new manager of Manchester City Pep Guardiola upon his arrival at the club:

'Have you got a coat with a hood on it? Cos you're gonna need it.'

(Mancity.com, July 2016)

Liam:

'I like characters – if the world was full of f*cking Gary Nevilles, it would be bobbins. He looks like an estate agent.'

(*Football Focus*, BBC1, April 2011)

Liam:

'I'm not having it . . .
[Wayne Rooney] . . . looks
like a f*cking balloon with
Weetabix crushed on top.'

(*Telegraph*, 2012)

Chapter 7

OASIS ON THE PRESS – WHAT'S THE STORY?

The Gallaghers were a press phenomenon in the 1990s and remain so to this day. Thirty years later, online or in print, you can't really avoid them and why would you want to, as the brothers remain as newsworthy and entertaining as ever? Liam and Noel are an interviewer's dream in that they are guaranteed to give you something funny, sensational and interesting. The only potential downside being if Liam takes a dislike to your cameraman.

Noel on music reviewers:

'I reckon if Thom Yorke f*cking shit into a light bulb and started blowing it like an empty beer bottle it'd probably get 9 out of 10 in f*cking *Mojo*.'

(*Esquire*, December 2015)

Liam on rock 'n' roll stories:

'There's more to being in a band
than writing songs, you know.
There's always something that
needs throwing out of the window,
someone who needs flicking
on the nose, and that line's
not going to snort itself.'

(*The Times*, June 2017)

Liam:

'I am a tender, beautiful and loving guy that happens to slap a photographer now and then because they get in my way.'

(Sky.com, July 2005)

Liam, when asked by a primary school kid, 'How do you deal with your anger management issues?':

'Ah interesting . . . Do you work for *The Sun*?'

(*Vice*, February 2018)

Liam on the press:

'I need them, need them to give me a kick up the arse. Otherwise I'd just be sat in getting fat, counting all me money. It's good [having] people living on your doorstep and looking through your bins. It gives you energy.'

(*NME*, July 1997**)**

Noel:

'Well, they're just waiting for us to make some monumental f*ck up, and they hope to be around when it happens. We've got to get one step ahead of those fellows.'

(*San Francisco Chronicle*, January 1998)

Noel:

'He's always going around saying,
"Why are they picking on me?"
and I'm going "Because you
go around punching
photographers in the face." '

(*NME*, July 1997)

Noel:

'I'd probably be incarcerated if
I was on Twitter . . . In interviews
I can always blame shit on you
[the journalist], I can always say
f*ck that guy, he twisted that shit.
If it's on my Twitter account
I'd end up in f*cking jail.'

(*National Post*, February 2015)

Liam:

'All that tabloid stuff is a pain in the arse, isn't it? I'd rather they wrote about me than some other dick. I'm interesting.'

(*NME*, July 1997)

Chapter 8

OASIS ON EVERYONE ELSE – SOME MIGHT SAY

What's fun about when Liam or Noel are on the promotion trail, is that they don't just have opinions on their fellow rock or pop stars. They can spout off about anyone. Yes, the Gallaghers are very much equal opportunity offenders. So, David Dickinson is as likely to get it as Dave Grohl. Samuel L. Jackson as Sam Smith. Royals, politicians, extra-terrestrials – no one is above getting a roasting from the brothers when they are fired up.

Noel:

'We like annoying people.
It's a Manchester thing. It's a trait.
We just like pissing people off.'

(*Rolling Stone*, May 1996)

Noel on meeting Tony Blair:

'I don't have a crystal ball. I didn't see he was going to turn into a c*nt. I was 30, off me head on drugs, and everyone telling me we were the greatest band since who knows. Then the prime minister invites you round for a glass of wine.'

(*SPIN*, October 2008)

Liam on Kanye West:

'If I ever win any more f*cking awards I'd personally invite him to get up and f*cking take my award off me . . . That was rude when he did that to that girl, that Taylor Swift. So yeah, give me an award and see where it goes.

It will roll out of his f*cking arse.'

(MTV's *120 Minutes*, August 2011)

Liam:

'I don't know what Brexit is,
all I know is that David Cameron
wants his b*llocks electrocuting
for bringing it on in the first place.'

(Q, June 2019)

Noel on Conservative politician
George Osborne:

'He might be the most slappable man in England, the kind of man that would watch *Coronation Street* or *EastEnders* to get a perspective on the working class.'

(*New Statesman*, October 2013)

Liam on whether he believes in aliens:

'Course I do. I'm not frightened by them, though, I'm as smart as them. Probably thick as f*ck, aren't they?'

(*NME*, July 1997)

Liam:

'My kids also like that bloke,
WhatsApp Ricky . . . [*when
told he means A$AP Rocky*]
Oh yeah, that's the fella.
WhatsApp Ricky. That's a better
f*cking name anyway.'

(GQ, July 2017)

Noel:

'I don't like workaholics.

Don't f*cking trust them.

Why are they working?

I don't trust busy c*nts.

That's how wars start: busy f*ckers.'

(*GQ*, October 2013)

Liam:

'It's like would Jesus Christ have been a f*cking pervert if he had a crisp packet on his head?'

(*i Paper*, September, 2019)

Noel:

'Prince Harry . . . f*cking asshole.
Just don't be f*cking dissing your
family because there's no need for it.'

(*Sun*, June 2021)

Chapter 9

OASIS ON EVERYTHING ELSE – ALL AROUND THE WORLD

So, when you've pretty much dissed *everyone*, what else is there left to insult? *Everything*, that's what. OK, Liam and Noel may soon have criticized nearly all of the nine billion humans that exist on Earth, but that still leaves cows, belts, mountains, bubble tea, e-scooters, meal deals . . . you get the idea. And when they've eviscerated everything on Earth, they can have a go at all the matter in the Universe. And after that I'm sure we'll be happy for them to get stuck into the Kaiser Chiefs and Gary Neville all over again.

Liam:

'F*ck the sea. I ain't going in that.
F*ck that, mate. That ain't meant for
us. That's meant for the sharks, and
the jellyfish, tadpoles and stuff.'

(*Vice*, August 2017)

Noel on The Priory:

'Why would you check into
a hospital to pay somebody
four grand an hour to tell you
things that really you should
already know about yourself?
. . . Give me the money.
I'll sort it out for you.'

(*Parkinson*, ITV, November 2006)

Liam:

'The Big Bang theory?
Not really a theory, is it?
What, one explosion and that was it?
Bit f*cking boring, if you ask me.'

(*GQ*, July 2017)

Liam:

'I try and beat the alarm clock.
The alarm goes off at six and
I try to get up at 5.59
just to do its head in.'

(BBC Radio 6 Music, February 2011)

Noel:

'Talking about the upping the ante,
when we get to South America,
we're going to set fire to some
bastard rainforests as well, man.
F*cking trees. Getting in
the way of all them car parks.'

(*E! News*, 1998)

Liam on nearly dying after eating M&Ms:

'That peanut, man, it nearly tipped me over the edge. It was a f*cking blue one and all, the cheeky bastard. I had a f*cking M&M and it felt like I'd been shot in the mouth.'

(*NME*, June 2013)

Liam on Glastonbury:

'It's just full of f*cking idiots.
It's like Bond Street with mud.'

(*Shortlist*, June 2011)

Noel:

'My laws would be: Smoke where you want, drink what you want, whenever you want . . . Anybody who wears a cowboy hat should get the electric chair.'

(*Rage*, September 1996)

Liam on pointy shoes:

'You know them shoes that come out at you like a f*cking snooker cue?! It's like, "leave it out man. You got a licence for them bastards or what?" '

(*Dazed & Confused*, 2009)

Noel on London riots:

'These fledgling democracies
in the Middle East, they're actually
fighting for their freedom.
And what are they rioting for in
England? Leisurewear.'

(*Telegraph*, October 2011)

Chapter 10

OASIS ON THEMSELVES – SUPERSONIC

After Oasis first burst into the public consciousness in 1994, declaring themselves 'the best group on the planet', they were characterized as arrogant. They laughed off such negativity – in fact, it seemed to fuel their self-belief. These guys were bulletproof, they even appeared arrogant about being arrogant. When Noel pronounces himself a genius there's always a twinkle in his eye, whereas when Liam declares himself 'godlike', he seems to truly believe it . . . as do many of us. Check out these immodest and biblical quotes.

Noel:

'. . . as God doesn't actually exist,
I'm afraid I'm gonna have to do
until someone better
qualified comes along'

(*GQ: Actually Me*, December 2017)

Noel:

'I'm not interested in making money.
It's just that with my talent,
I'm cursed with it.'

(*SPIN*, October 2008)

Liam:

'If you're not confident then you're a
f*cking bag of pork scratchings.'

(*Oasis Uncut*, MTV Europe, December 1997)

Noel:

'Here's what you do: you pick up your guitar, you rip a few people's tunes off, you swap them round a bit, get your brother in the band, punch his head in every now and again and it sells.'

(*Observer*, September 1995)

Liam:

'Stone Roses 1989.
I was in the crowd and I thought
f*ck this, I'm off to do it myself.'

(*Telegraph*, August 1997)

Liam:

'I suppose I do get sad,
but not for too long. I just look in
the mirror and go, "What a f*cking
good-looking f*ck you are."
And then I brighten up.'

(*NME*, 2006)

Noel:

'Has God played
Knebworth recently?'

(*NME*, July 1997)

Liam:

'If I wasn't a musician
I don't know. I'd be God, maybe?
That would be a good job.'

(*Sun*, 2005)

Noel:

'There's not a day goes by that I don't, y'know, that I don't think f*cking hell, we did something really spectacular there. I still can't articulate what it was, d'you know what I mean, because it was more, although it was the songs and all that, it was more than that though, it was more than that.'

(*Take 5* interview with Zan Rowe, ABC Radio, October 2023)

Liam:

'They think I'm a big-mouthed
c*nt from Manchester,
and they'd be correct.'

(*Clash*, October 2008)

ACKNOWLEDGEMENTS

Publisher: Trevor Davies
Copy Editor: Caroline Taggart
Art Director: Mel Four
Illustrator: Simon Spilsbury
Senior Production Manager: Peter Hunt